SWALLOWS IN DECEMBER

JEROME KIELY

Note for Librarians: A cataloguing record for this book is available from Library and Archives Canada at www.collectionscanada.ca/amicus/index-e.html
ISBN 1-4120-6404-x

Printed in Victoria, BC, Canada. Printed on paper with minimum 30% recycled fibre. Trafford's print shop runs on "green energy" from solar, wind and other environmentally-friendly power sources.

TRAFFORD

Offices in Canada, USA, Ireland and UK

This book was published *on-demand* in cooperation with Trafford Publishing. On-demand publishing is a unique process and service of making a book available for retail sale to the public taking advantage of on-demand manufacturing and Internet marketing. On-demand publishing includes promotions, retail sales, manufacturing, order fulfilment, accounting and collecting royalties on behalf of the author.

Book sales for North America and international:
Trafford Publishing, 6E–2333 Government St.,
Victoria, BC v8t 4p4 CANADA
phone 250 383 6864 (toll-free 1 888 232 4444)
fax 250 383 6804; email to orders@trafford.com
Book sales in Europe:
Trafford Publishing (uk) Ltd., Enterprise House, Wistaston Road Business Centre,
Wistaston Road, Crewe, Cheshire cw2 7rp UNITED KINGDOM
phone 01270 251 396 (local rate 0845 230 9601)
facsimile 01270 254 983; orders.uk@trafford.com
Order online at:
trafford.com/05-1315

10 9 8 7 6 5 4 3 2

For the Friends who did not walk away.

Contents

PEOPLE

COUSIN FIONÁN

Fionán went to bed with books
when he was seven
and stayed cohabiting
with their sensuous spines
till he was seventy.

Then one summer's day
a torrent of dammed up desire
swept him out of his bookcased gorge
to a lake where a girl
naked as an end page
climbed out upon an illustrated shore.

Inside three months
all the books in the bed
were on the floor
and her rounded mouth
was the only capital letter
in his life.

FUNERAL MAN

The mart is our Redeemer
and football our bright Paraclete
but the funeral is the Father
in our social Trinity.

Every town has funerals
but only ours has Jimmy:
he walks in front of every hearse
from church to burial place.

In an age of discreet mourners
riding in evasive cars
his deviating presence
keeps funerals in walking shoes.

What horses' hooves did once
for reverence, his feet do now;
the gearshift of his will
keeps every car in first.

Coffins are inarticulate
but his slow steps express
the graciousness of lunacy,
the shabbiness of sense.

Jimmy is our minesweeper
clearing the explosive streets;

the cortege of the cars a line
of battleships astern.

"Jimmy is coming" is the cry
that anaesthetises stores;
windows lose their consciousness,
the mouths of doors fall slack.

Level with his shoulders he
extends two planks of arms
as he processionals the cross
down the aisle of silent shops

and thus he paces gate to gate,
distraction between prayer and prayer,
secular parenthesis
in a priestly paragraph.

Our sole egalitarian
he does equal honour
to the iridescent casket
moulded in a bank vault

and to the white deal coffin
easy gnaw for maggots
foetus from a tree
at the back of a council house.

DIRK

Her garden
is a Kremlin
where the onions are inviolate
as cyrillic domes.

To protect them
against jackdaws
she laces bread with poison, and
great black leaves fall.

Unmissably
she mornings Mass
and takes the Maker of all life
in killer hands.

Demolisher
of spiders' webs
she will not let the weavers work
her dahlia looms.

Not God Himself
may claim a flower;
each bloom is pinned like medal on
her martial chest.

Hatred of her
won't bring back life

but Verse gives me the gaelic dirk
to slay the slayer.

WHY?

We found him hanging stiffly
like the pendulum
of a stopped clock.
The mechanism of habit
had finally run down.
Around his neck like a constricting snake
there was a loop of red electric wire.
A raw and purple lump of flesh
which was his tongue but yesterday
gluttoned the open mouth.
We crossed ourselves and looked away.

Everybody knew he was a foreigner
who bought the land to farm for Irish peace:
if so, what need had he to plough
the plot of death to crop it?
What noises vexed the stranger's dream?
Was it that doubts were drumming
in the future mind, or had he heard
the silence shouting in suspicious eyes?
Eternal rest grant unto him, O Lord.

Some people blamed the dwellinghouse
squatting like an injured toad among the trees;
some blamed the trees themselves,
closeranked like troops
to guard this bivouac of gloom

against the sun. Six hundred rooks
home in on them like a tornado twist,
and in the night the waiting owls
open their terrifying sudden eyes
like Inquisition monks who lift their fearsome cowls.

"WHERE ARE YOU?" ADAM SPEAKING

When the sun became ashamed
of its flashing nakedness
and made itself an apron of red leaves
emptily west of our Eden stand of trees,
it was then God took His planet walk.
Knowing everything without benefit of fruit
He knew that evening was a time apart
for sowing closeness, sprinkling talk
and tilling of the human heart.
There were four rivers that our garden tamed
but when He looked in them to see a face
there were four vacant mirrors.
He found Himself in us; with Eve and me
He sought another trinity.
To be level with our level, visible like us
and visibly beautiful as Eve for that He came
the evening of His walk. But there's one thing
God cannot do: to cease to be Himself,
invisible, invisibly most beautiful.
"Where are you?", He called out. I heard the pain
of God, the pain of knowing we could greet
each other from a distance, but not meet.

Now when my brow is pocked with sweaty clay
Eden is a mirage away;
our rivers which we thought flowed to some sea
have burrowed like the scorpions into sand;

always in our minds there is that worm
slithering in the mucus of desire,
and where there was an orchard of the eye
now there is a graveyard on our land
with only stumps of apples skeletoned and dry.
I never hear Him walking in the drill
behind me, never clutch
to the belief that it is He has kissed our tent
when the lips of oxen leather part and touch.
When if ever will His evening cool?
Sometimes we see Him in a rainbow or a dove
but every sighting is a clothed God;
our longing is to touch Him naked, bare,
stripped of every other thing but love.
"Where are You?" we call out in greater pain
than when the anguish comes on Eve
than when the lion mangles limb
because our pain is now the pain of Him
who cried "Where are you?" knowing we can greet
Him from a distance but not meet.

AUNTIE

She went to the wedding in black:
clothes are contemporaries.
But weddings are breeders of wit
and the witty asked whether it meant
she expected a death.

The groom called her Auntie from when
his father named all of the world:
the gimlet, the soldering blower,
the hacksaw, the pint and the keys
and Auntie next door.

She biscuited kitchen for him,
let him slalom down bottoming stairs
and when she ringed him around
in a circle of squeezebox and arms
she was the best of all players.

She was eighty the day David wed
but her squeezebox was supple as youth
and when the band called for a truce
and silenced their drummed cannonade
it was time that she played.

She sat at the edge of the stage
with her eyes on her sinuous tunes.
Some said "She is great for her years"

then remembered the war they'd been through
and went off to their beers.

No one told her stage turns were old hat
that her obsolete love was not needed,
but the past was strapped on to her hands
and she carried on playing for the boy
unheard and unheeded.

KISSING A CORPSE

You were too late in coming. Candle
pulsed for a seized-up heart.
How could she see with eyes that were coffined
under stretched lids? The mart
for trading life's regrets had closured;
you and she are worlds apart.

You came too late, too late to shatter
a wall you built with blocks of hate.
There was no calendar where you could cancel
your next appointed bitter date.
Death amputates the hand that could have
picked the lock on her shut gate.

You kissed her cheek: what use is kissing
dead cheek that freezes frozen lips?
those lips of yours that lacerated
her ailing flesh with cutting quips.
The candle shivered; did you fathom
its icy, helled apocalypse?

THE CYCLIST (1936)

The road that magicked out of town
was called the Eastern Road, and led
to wonders like the Taj Mahal
that I had fetched from shelves
stretch high in the Junior Library.
It also gobbled up my father
at teatime every cycling Sunday
but funned him back to me
on summer Saturdays
when I was noosed by bike and arms
within a tight lasso of love.

I only knew one way to stretch
a welcome with a boyish hand:
I climbed on the back of the Eastern Road
till it put me down on the cross for Cork
and there I sat on Coleman's ditch
with eyes like telescopes
counting the craters of the buttercups,
and waiting for the tinkle of a thumb
on the bell that would tell my eager ears
that wheels were chasing the lively sounds.
Then he appeared iconing the brow
glorious as the tin advertisement
for Raleigh bikes on Mylie Murphy's door.

Reunion was another name

for the crossbar where he lifted me;
and in the cuddled circle
of arms and handlebars
I gauged the heat of scorching tyres
as we freewheeled to the town a mile away
leaning against him like a quayside ship,
eyes shut against the summer flies,
heart open to the weekly rush of love.

BURIAL OF A WOMAN OF THE OLD STOCK

Down along the ebbing laneway
lurching to the graveyard and the sea
they shouldered Annie's coffin.
It was varnished like a new canoe.
More people than she ever knew
came to see the launching.

Half a cable inland from the shore
lay the hulk of a battered church:
two centuries before the English gunners
gave their corvine kin an entrance
her people roofed it for the psalter.

When the bearers bowed and went inside,
the walls stood up erect;
then they placed her coffin on the trestles
in the very chancel, of all sacred places:
it was the same as setting up an altar.

The mourners entered and at once
stepped out of the footwear of their talk
and stood in silence. Through a window
slender as a lance Longinus peered,
and on the ground next to the open grave
there was a mound of fine grained earth
the sainted powder of four hundred years.

There are strong farmers buried in a bog
and bishops inside concrete bunkers.

Outside the ring of friends
outside the folded arms of church
there was a third enclosure.
This was a lios of circling fog
a rath enclosing as raths always did
people and cattle, life and death.

Beyond it, there was no world to be seen;
within it, was a world of reverence
and at the centre of that quiet world
there was a coffin, an altar, a canoe
and a woman of the old stock, through and through.

"FOR O, FOR O, THE HOBBY HORSE IS FORGOT."

Fishermen lowered a barrel of his praises:
he was the one who lobstered all their pots
and steered the weekly francs from Roscoff.

Republicans reread the faded Tan War pages:
he was the one who ovened armoured cars
and lit the winter night with barracks.

He built the Hall; the dancers waxed his maple;
all the laughs in plays were his, the shouts in pool;
in that new world he was Columbus.

The clergy paid their dues with panegyrics;
when depth of pocket measured height of spire
for their new church his hand dug deepest.

The children lined his coffin way with lightness
for in the annals of abandoned school
his was the only funeral to free them.

But he was the last one of his race at Shanagh,
and six years on, the hobby horse is forgot
and his grave is thicketed with briars.

AT A FUNERAL HOME

Take the winding bands from off your feet
and stop your sorrow shuffle:
that is not a coffin you are looking at
but a canoe.
If what you heard about the boy were true,
if life's schoolteaching could not tutor him
to count beyond eleven
the undertaker would have laid the body flat,
not shoulderwedged against the coffin's back
with bright head resting on the rim.

Did I say rim? No, that's the gunwale,
and what you see as satin ruffing
is spume thrown up by hurtle hull.
The wreaths upon the floor which florists culled
for innocence are no such thing
but water whitened by uprushing rocks.
And what you itemise as rosary and rose
are steering lines his taut hands grip
and mascot motherpinned upon his clothes.

So leave your handshake hands outside the door
(sprung coils of pain: what else are they?)
and stand with me close to the torrents' cheek
drenched not by tears but thrilling spray:
the little lad shoots rapids down the day.

BROTHER PRIESTS

They stood together on multiples of tees
from where their eyes got bunkered on a hill
and fairwayed down a lake.

They preached from one another's lecterns
to put their hobby horses out to grass
for one week in the clichéd year.

The only thing that ever stood between them
in the years before the priesthood vinegarred
was a bottle that was speaking vivid French.

They were at their team togethered best
not at a High Mass when, as like as not,
they genuflected when they should have bowed

but in an eighteen footer in a race
when they would be two carpenters
planing the jib and mainsail stiff as board.

They broke no medieval lances over tomes
but argued half their lives which pet was best:
a setter after snipe, or cat on rug.

They were like brothers till the gospel put
a fratricidal weapon in their hearts.
"I was in prison but you never came

to see me" were Christ's killing words,
and when one of their own was locked away
they let him quote them, and they never went.

BEACHCOMBER

A man bulges from the shadows –
the misanthropic gulls are vexed.
A knapsack sways in the contour of his back
like a monkey on its mother,
and in his hands he carries
the offspring of his hopes
a creature with a discus head
and a body long as a vaulting pole.
Peel away that skin of imagery
and the hard fruit is a detector.

The man is an evening alchemist
turning the metal losses of the day
into his pinch of gold.
He goes to work with all the care
of a sapper in a minefield
missing no inch of where
the fallible beachpeople were.

Therefore he searches in the sandy keep
of the English boy's Caernarvon,
and all along the catwalk
where the youths who lost themselves
watching the walking swimwear
might have lost a silver lighter,
and in the updraft dunes
where men with falcon souls

had kited with the wind
and might have lost their footing
in the world of euros,
but mostly where the women who had spread
their marriage fat on hired sunbeds
had dropped, perhaps, the cocktail change
through leaky fingers
or hid an earring irritant
under a forgotten mattress.

He bows profoundly
when a miracle occurs and thereupon
the monkey on his back chortles.

CREATURES

CATERPILLAR

I am not strong
on caterpillars.

I can tell an avocet
sweeping its scythe
to harvest worms,
from an oystercatcher
drilling for molluscs
with brace and bit,
and I can tell an oak
stolid as a patriarch,
from a flamboyant birch
all gamy legs and arms,
but when it comes
to caterpillars
I have no expertise
to tell which make
a concertina is.

The caterpillar
that stopped the garden breathing
had a sestet of strange eyes,
two for seeing
and four for mesmerising,
and when it moved
on paps that were its legs
its head exploded

in a proboscis.

As it lurched
across the gravel path
it looked like covered wagons
negotiating a ravine
but when it reached the lawn
a coast-to-coast railroad express
thrust through the prairie grass.

"What was it, Edna?"
I asked my friend
whose volumed head
is my rare library.
"Elephant hawkmoth
at a guess", she said,
"but when I bring
you Richard South on moths
you'll know for sure".

South gave a full page plate
to what I saw:
a trunk-propelling snout,
mammalian legs,
intimidating painted eyes.
The letters of its name stood up,
they raised their arms,
they capitally roared
ELEPHANT HAWKMOTH
CATERPILLAR.

He added in his text
"When in repose,
the head and foremost rings
are inward drawn
and this distends
the discs of decoy eyes
thus bringing them
into great prominence
and giving the creature
a very wicked look".

I beg to differ, Richard.
Not wicked.
Baleful, rather.
There is a wizard world
of difference.

DYSFUNCTIONAL ROBIN

Robin,
halfway to redbreast
I fear you never
will don the jerkin.

Today he flouted
Fan Ann the huntress
in a downpour of sparrows
for a sprinkle of cake.

That's what comes of watching
staid Solemn Sammy
when finches go raiding
at his outpost of tail.

He hasn't completed
a course of logic
and erringly argues
from particular to general.

Erithacus rubecula
is a solitary eater
and should leave the table
at the whirr of sparrows,

but not this robin:
if he sees them rucking

he's in there hooking
for an oval crumb

and when he's there first
he refuses to be
intimidated
by noise or numbers.

Inhibition
is the topic he skipped
in the handbook they give
to juvenile birds.

Robin,
I beg of you
be like the Christians
loving all and trusting none.

LADYBIRD

When the ladybird landed
on my index finger nail
she sembled a sexchange
in the husk of a male

and the nail became an orchestra
a smooth Greek dancing place
and the insect a warrior dancer
moving with martial grace

round and round in the sunlight
till my eyes in the theatre reeled
watching the seven black bosses
wheel on his amber shield.

Once he walked up the parodos
the finger's passageway
but loathed the feel of spectators,
their flesh, rushed back, said nay

to rabble, dancing in armour,
the artist, soldier, sage
and solitary, loving
the grand autocracy of stage.

IMAGES OF GOD

A white leaf tumbled from a tree
but never hit the ground:
it fell from God's taut forestry
where Butterflies abound.

A shard of glass took wings and flew
down Little Brosna's stream:
God's was the kiln that fired the blue
that makes Kingfishers gleam.

With ebbing day a rust red ship
muzzled through waves of grass:
no one but God was on the slip
which launched that Fox's class.

MESSAGE FOR THE GATHERERS OF LEAVES

Dancing partners of the garden rake,
proselytisers of fallen leaves,
burners of the autumn turncoats,
manicurists to your meretricious lawns,
I have a message for you.
It is the message of the Lord to Moses:
"Do not strip the vineyard bare
or cut the corn to the edges of the field".

When next the black gauleiter in your hearts
has targeted the leaves for ethnic cleansing
make out a Schindler's list,
spare some of them;
we have enough of Dachaus and Treblinkas.
The rooks will need them for the nests of March
to cover their twig cots with blankets
and drape the draughty walls
of nurseries
with autumn woven tapestries.

You have no time for rooks, you say,
autumn, spring or any roosting hour.
That's not the issue here.
The issue is: the rook is class,
his family are the Corvidae
and surely you don't wish

to be discredited
by the brightest, aptest, most intelligent
of all the creatures God has made
after dolphins, chimpanzees and us.

DOOMED CREATURES

An upside down electric shade
is called a fitting, nothing else,
but in my winter bedroom I
am calling it the well of woe
for at the bottom is a wasp
imprisoned by his impotence.

When I switch on the warming light
the wasp goes orbiting the sun
but when my finger schedules sleep
it brings about a full eclipse:
the planet dies, the dark invades
the heart, the dinosaur lies cold.

Each night the kiss of light revives
the wasp but only for as long
as I undress; when those lips freeze,
the concentration camp regime
silences its cries for help
and drops it in a flightless hell.

I watch myself as well as wasp
inside that lamp: half respite comes
through sea, wine, image, cat or friend
but I am pitched into a well
where wings can't whirr. Though wasp may glint
in amber bowl it dies in jar of sand.

BILLY DIVER

We called him Billy Diver
threepal William, Donie and myself
when we were free of minding shop
watching from the barelegged harbour wall.
We loved the leap he made
into the twisting air
before he scimitared the water,
and the thistlehead that grew upon the surface
out of his long deep stem.

Without a watch between us
we measured the vast reams
of time he stayed submerged
with William doing it by jabbing air
and Donie by a finger on his pulsing wrist
and I by penduling my ticking head
and got all different answers as in school.
Then when he stood on a triumphant rock
gesticulating with an athlete's arms
we used to think he did it
to acknowledge our acclaim.

Then came the facts in books:
there were Divers properly so called,
Great Northerns, White Billed and Black Throated (rare);
he wasn't one of them, our cormorant;
he was a jawbreak *Phalacrocorax*

belonging to a family different from theirs:
might as well call a Regan Barrett
or a Barrett Kiely as call him Diver.
What's more, he didn't stay submerged heroic minutes;
thirty seconds was an average dive.
He wasn't driven by our thirst of fun
but by his gorging lust for eels, and when
he made the rock a rostrum, as we thought,
it was in fact to dry his sodden wings
and in politest language to
eject the pellets of undigested food.

The adolescence of reality
arrived one day when his big eyes
had trouble swallowing his fish.
He broke the surface with an eel
round as a cycle tube,
sinuous as our Sunday ties.
He shook it in the way that Donie's terrier
would shake a rat and used the surface
like a thwart to smash its head on;
he tossed it, caught it, sluiced it through
the dual turbines of his throat and neck,
then swam to a latrine of rock.
It was a gauche performance: he had left
the high olympics of the diving board
and joined a circus of low appetites.

How I wish he were again
the Billy Diver of my innocence

who somersaulted to excite his fans
and held his suicidal breath
to break the world endurance record,
and how I wish that it were still   ·
before the era of the book restraints
before the bullying of facts had cowed the mind
and that William, Donie and myself
were let off minding shop –
just watching him.

PILLAR

I called him Pillar
because that is where he sat
every begging day
either bringing his terracotta figure
to my unartistic gate
when sun encouraged sculpture
or else his draggle
in the pleading rain.

The stray cat lived
in some uncharted waste of fear
east of my appled Eden
for always as he came and went
he walked on shortened legs
belly to protective ground
like an infantry recruit
skulking from an ambuscade.

When I appeared
with answers on a plate
he dropped down from the pillar,
the lookout of his fort,
on to the parapet
and watched the vanguard of relief
through an embrasure in the wall
like the lone legionnaire
in a remembered childhood film.

Each purring day
the buttons of his eyes
fastened their bright discs
through the slitted buttonholes of mine
and, once he stretched a human paw
to touch my feline fingertip
like Adam meeting God
in Michelangelo.

But tombs grow out of gardens
even in the case of God,
and on a Thursday night
when Pillar was returning
to his squatter's shack
a car's psychotic eyes
mesmerised the darkness
into killing him.

Next day I chanced upon him
on the pounded street
like a discarded teacosy.
My fort is abandoned and
my sculpture razed.

A LUCKY ROBIN GIVES AN INTERVIEW

Robin, the sparrow gossips tell me that
you had a brush with death.

I query your word "brush": a panther's teeth
are not what I'd call bristles.

Ah now, robin, why exaggerate?
The sparrows say it was the curate's cat
dressed in the cleric clothes.

Black cat to him, but how does he scale up
to rhino? Does he call it cow?
She had eyes like yellow plates: her nose
had two nests gaping side by side.
I swear by the winged Man who died
and bloodied my breast feathers I was mauled
by an Asian panther.

Let it pass.
But how do you, most circumspect of birds
with head like swivelled radarscoop explain
how you were caught off guard?

Atlantic rain,
that's how. The downpour fell in drapes.
How could I see through cloaks that camouflaged
the panther's lair in the hydrangeas?

Besides, we're not our best in rain: we look
like altarboys at funerals on drenching days
with rivulets of hair and sodden capes.

I take your point, but can you tell me why
you were present on that garden path ... I mean
the forest floor where panthers stalk.

I can.
That damn fool of a priesting man
who likes to reconstruct the bible scene
should spread his manna on a crest
not on the ground. That was my mistake,
to lower my sky brain to his madeira cake.
Thinking with the stomach is not wise.
That's how the panther got me.

What a shock
that must have been for you.

The blackest fright
I ever got! Teeth like a portcullis
closed on my gate of life; a wrestler's lock
lifted me off my feet; death slobbered me a kiss.
Only that the panther had acquired the knack
of carrying her cubs by gentle scruff, my plight
would have been worse – a death by garrotting.
I praise the Saviour for remembering
the thorn my forebear plucked out of His head
when He was facing death.

Amen to that.
But how did you escape your Roman cat?

She rated me a trophy for her priest
a bottled curio on his mantelpiece
and bounded in the open petting door,
but he no sooner saw my piteous state
than he lashed her with one great whipping roar.
"Panther!" he screamed.

"Fan Ann!" is what he said.

Quickly she flinched and dropped me on the floor.
That was my chance; I took it with a whirr.
Three walls were bricked with books, the fourth was bright
with robin world, a hedge, a tree, the sky.
I made a thrust for that, but wham!
The air was solid, a translucent wall.
I think that was the biggest shock of all.

You hit a window, robin.

Window? Yes, by God
it winded me. Dazed as a duck, I was
fluttering on the floor. Never again will I
scoff at the wobbly bats because at least
they have a way with walls; better them
with wings like leather leaves than me
with a bill like a stubbed in bow
on a yacht that goes tilting at a quay.

How is it now?

Still skewways as you see.

But you recovered, you got out. I've heard it said
you robins have a spool of Ariadne's thread
for getting out of labyrinths.

Nothing as magical as that. The manna man,
keeper of panthers, priest of the Most High
lowered a cage he made of ten white claws
and clamped me in it, I surely thought to die,
but God be praised and blessed he lifted me
in that tight cage across the yowling room
and out the door. O, liberty!
He pulled the bars apart, I frenzied free
across the hedge, the tree, the homing sky
and heard the glad rain beating on the drums
and left the sparrows browsing on the crumbs.

PLACES

BALLABUIDHE HORSE FAIR

Ponies to horses
are like foothills to mountains;
the ears of the tallest
climb sheer to twin summits.

From the Square to Pat Mollie's
handlers pace out seduction;
there are grunts of acceptance
and smiles of refusal.

Cluster of ponies
modelled by patience
linked by neck arches
are fit for a carver.

A man stretches friendship
six pints from his shoulder
and the raffle, praise God, is
a tierce of black porter.

There are boots up on stakes like
pitched heads of hung traitors.
Balloons are on sale, big
as lobster pot markers.

Children on shoulders
children on ponies

compete for a view of
men hedge hogged on nailbeds.

The pubs are as full as
the Metro at rush-hour
and outside there are hunters
hitched to foglamps and mudguards.

Sounds of steam railways
track the spun wheel-of-fortune.
Eyes ride with nostalgia
on the Travellers' piebalds.

The hands of spectators
are chopped off by pockets
and the girls nod to palmists
as in open confession.

There are manes with the trimness
of Afric-chic hairdos
and manes that cascade like
a winter-spurred torrent.

And a lover of beauty
eyes wide as a harem
vows "I'll buy a whole hundred
when I lasso the Lotto."

ONE YOUNG SUMMER

Seablue days
with only a small regatta of cloud.
Street pals William and myself
cycled to King Charles Fort
and left our bikes in the custody
of a sleeping motte.

We crossed the footbridge over the stream
- it gave the harbour the shivers -
so small the simple arch
could have been a niche for a statue
and along the path to Middle Cove
tracker file – that's all the space there was –
between farmers' meanness on the left
and sea's offlimits on the right.
There was a section where
you didn't see farmers' or harbour's furrows
when we entered a tunnel
roofed and walled by blackthorn;
and another where the coastal rocks
cared nothing for the farmers' notices
and trespassed barefoot on their fields;
and a gully where the tide came
and went with different voices
tenor coming and deep bass going.

When, last corner, the beach beamed

and the path plunged
to finger its face
there was a rock
hulled like a caravel
that we called the "Santa Maria"
and we leaped from the prow
to claim El Salvador
for God and Spain and our selfish selves;
then changing roles to Indian skin
we sat and swimming togged.

The cove was a letter W
and navigating by whatever wind that blew
we havened and we swam
in the eastern or the western U.
Enough of water play, we searched
the shore for keyhole limpet shells
but didn't think too highly
of the conchologist who named them such;
we called them volcano craters
hats with ventilators
wigwams with a hole for smoke.
Afterwards we stole away
like corncrakes to a meadow
and keeping within earshot of our argument
but out of sight in modest nests
we sunbathed for a naked hour.

The year was nineteen forty one
and like the limpet shells

the world had lost its hold.
We too, united though we were
by age and street and two oar boat,
were uncoupled by the War,
for William's dad had paced a deck
painted Royal Navy grey
and I was blooded on
the torn flesh of Ninety Eight,
so on the day the cove became a camera
our eyes and ears became belligerents,
for out of a sky smoothed for swimming
a Stuka bomber dived
south of the Old Head's exclamation mark
in neutral glitter
on an old freighter bound for Liverpool.
William prayed the Germans' dive
became their ditching
and I willed them a medal
from the Führer's hand.

Ceasefire declared, though not in Russia,
one thing for sure brought full agreement,
the time the hunger clock struck go.
Then we left Columbus beached,
listened again for bass or tenor,
blackthorn blacker in the tunnel,
challenged Charles and crossed the stream
feet on granite
thoughts on grotto.
Our bikes acclaimed

the seventh commandment,
and on we leapt
without benefit of pedal
togs dangling from the handlebars
drying for another wetting
back to Kinsale
with its head in the sun
and shoulders in shadow,
downhill from Hendersons
singeing the screaming tyres
flaunting freewheel arabesques,
owning the road.

STATION MASS AT HEIR ISLAND

The bow of the boat kept its hands joined;
wood through water muttered prayer;
the eye of the tiller never looked
at gannet gestures showing where
the Station morning mackerel were.

A cottage knelt above the cove.
With brisk faith windolened its bright
eyes watched the priest get off the boat
and satchel-carry up the height
a future God, calm, waferlight.

Handshakes crossplanked the door with peace
and when priest entered first names boomed,
the chairs clicked heels, the grate-plant flamed
and all the eyes sailed up the room
where table was awash with crochet spume.

Candles lighthoused, flowers broached,
ceiling kissed the chalice lips.
William, three, tried Jacob's stairs
but the angel had his wild wings clipped.
Silence savoured the sacred sips.

When Mass was finished we sat outside.
The cat of Cléire watched us eat,
its ears cliff-high, its back hill-humped,

and stretched out in the purring heat
two promontory paws in front of it.

We went home by the western rocks,
monastic, calm, liturgical;
the Benedictine cormorants
spread out black sleeves in common call
on God from their ancient choir stalls.

MALLABRACKA

My eye is steady as a camera.
Angle, wide.
Courtesy of evening
I have lighting from the side.

Dunnes' cows are moving
hither and over
like pendulum clocks telling the time
to the leisurely clover.

On the Togher road
there are bungalows
white walls black windows
playing dominoes.

I can't see the Bandon
but swans on the energetic wing
with necks like teachers' pointers show
every twist and turn of the vacillating thing.

Centre picture
is a wonderment of rock.
Egypt, surely. Aren't they step pyramids?
For all I care, geologists can mock.

And the top of my frame is a purple sofa
called Sheha Mountain where legends sit

and a hanging of sky richly clouded
at the back of it.

GARLAND SUNDAY

The wells are where the ancient gods –
once openly and nationally ours,
long hidden in their fear of croziers –
show their heads,
and once a year we bring them wreaths of flowers.

The pilgrims go and climb the Reek
not to nurse the Christian tumour at the peak
but to retrace
the veins upon that aged face.

Children blued and basketed
up where the hillsides hoot in flurries
stretch fingers back three thousand years
to gather whortleberries.

And people in from the monkish rocks
cast off their melancholy smocks
tailored by minds that were beehive cells
and stamp their pagan glee
upon the sensual platform of the quay.

SUMMER LAKE UNDER
NABHANN MOUNTAIN

When I look up at Nabhann's crest
I am an entomologist:
I see a long white centipede of cloud
scurrying where scurrying is not allowed
across the hostile summitry of rock.

From there as I look down at Cullenach
I am an ophthalmologist:
the lake is my patient's eye with a cataract of mist.

Half distance down the elegant slope
I open up a jeweller's shop
and loop a necklace of a torrent round
a neck of steep aristocratic ground.

Tiring of work I take an image break
and holiday the shoreline of the lake
where unseen ducks in squabbling weeds
syringe the silent ears, and reeds
like a disciplined mosque of Friday brether
raise and bend their heads together.

Then a swallow takes charge of my imaging eyes
and angles the surface dapping for flies
and skims like a playstone five times in a row
but never like my stone plummets below.

Last, two youngsters arrive with shy togs in their hands
and wonder to God when that fool of a man
with his pencil and paper will please go away
so as they can dip summer on this summer's day.

CARRAIG MHÓR AN tSIONNAIGH

My downstairs eyes
could see nothing of the sunspread world
except a wall without a window.
The Polyphemus of geology
had rolled this rock
to make my living room a tomb
and kill the life of sea and mountain
and so the first name that I christened it
in the naming language of the country was
Carraig Chonstaice
which being translated is Obstruction Rock.

My upstairs eyes
looked out of children's sockets.
The landing was a schoolroom not a tomb;
the window was my manual
where I memorised the capital
letters of God's alphabet:
the apexed A of Púca Mountain
the curling C of Ballydevlin Bay
the pronging E
of Castle, Weave and Ballydevlin Points.
The rock became a writing slate
that I discarded;
that's why I named it at the second call
Carraig In Aisce.
Rock of No Account.

And then one upstairs morning
before Mass bell or the cattle truck
the letters were no longer capitals.
When I looked out, the worthless rock
was grander than the Mountain
far more exclamatory than the Bay
more mystic than the trident of the Points
for standing on the crest
there was a fiery fox
sculpted on a plinth
daring in his beauty
the pinnacle of life
the sunup of the morning with a brush of cloud.
One moment he was there; the next, was gone;
he didn't leave with what you'd call
a trot, a lope, a stalk;
it was as if a presence evanesced,
and for the first time in my sceptic life
I put my faith in apparitions.
Now the mighty rock is named for him
definitively
and for all poetic time
Carraig Mhór an tSionnaigh.

LIVING AND
PARTLY LIVING

WHISKEY PUNCH

Winter's supremest joy, the swig of punch
leaves bed unbulged
for downstairs at the alcoholic hearth
the fire paints Impressionist
pictures of the demons in the drink,
the whiskey chortles as it jumps
into a heated pool of glass
and the kettle's boiling cataract
abets sweet suicide of sugar.

WALK THROUGH SPRING

I saw the river and a country road
keeping company.
Prurient I made it three,
but in less than half a happy mile
the river took exception to my smile
and sulked, and sighting shields
of sycamores ran off
across a chastity of fields,
leaving me to amble with the road alone
at a frustrated bend.

"Cut your loss, it's not the end
of walking into spring" a songthrush called
and plain world green became Irish emerald.

So I miled and miled again
and three times miled
and passed six houses with processions
of daffodils from gates to doors
in double files
the farmers' annual flirtation
with the femininity of flowers;
and I stopped at a boutique
where primroses were displaying parasols;
and got a lesson from a sgeach
on physiology
for all the buds were little penises

and every penis showed a Hebrew glans –
not a solitary gentile could I see
from Beersheba to Dan.

Then I came across a metamorphosis
when ivy clambered up a telepole
and made of it a great green lolly,
but the sight that really arched a bridge
across the river Tantrum
and its alluvial melancholy
was a cat stretched out in the ginger sun
on the saddle of a snoozing motor bike;
that, and the counter of Cotter's bar
where a discursive Heineken described
to Tom and Ted the walk through spring
no winter gone could mar
but with never a mention of that Hebrew tribe!

PRAYER BEFORE COMMUNION

Do not come to me in the visibility of bread:
I do not want a pennyworth of You
on a begging palm,
I do not want to cast
a discus of You
into the stadium of my mouth,
I do not want You to dissolve
upon my tongue
quicker than the cheapest sweet.
I want Your richness, not a coin,
I want Your triumph, not a quoit,
I want to taste Your company
not a sodden mess.

Come in the sinuosity of wine
which will wriggle
through the forest of my flesh.
Come in the swirl of wine
which has neither a beginning nor an end
so I can cask infinity.
Come in the majesty of wine
to which I have to tilt my head
so I can drink submissively.
Come in the redness vintaged by
a Gothic window looking west.
Come with the energy
crushed from a hundred suns.

PASSAGE UNDER SAIL

We waited in the masted air
bent like hairpins on the yards
until the skipper gave the order "loose the sails!"
Then we let fall all of the barque's fair hair.

The sails filled out with a salvo sound of guns
and Rob recalled how there in Santa Cruz
one naphtha noon Drake had a man-of-war
blown to Catholic hell by the hidalgos' sons.

We set a slamming course for Tenerife,
lee scuppers gargling with ocean salt, and shrouds
using a saw upon the shrieking sky;
we praised the elemental God of child-belief.

Astern we left the mountains sitting down;
ahead of us were rising alps of cloud;
across the blue glen in between we sailed
the sea leagues of Columbus's renown.

A crescent dolphin lit the dark below;
four dolphin sickles cut great tracts of sea;
torpedoes aimed their joy; and, joy,
our dolphin-striker never struck a blow.

Abeam of us we made of speed and spray
a spread of lace for sea's jade table top

and on this lace we set our vessel down,
the lovely ornament of an earlier day.

ROUTE TO THE BUTTERFLIES

I'll tell you where the butterflies are
wavery masses of butterflies are
like drunken tanglers at Ballabuidhe fair
staggering from holly to furze to thorn
nettles to sloe to crocheted fern.

Leave your car at Donovan's Castle
host to seven stragglers of sky
and walk grasseasy up the middle of the road
on a bulge of sod which has buried the tarmac
to your first marker: it's a bed of meadow
where a foal with legs stretched out inert
like polished furniture lies asleep
under the canopy of his mother's care.

Next you will come to the theatre quarter
with a festival of fuchsia dangling puppets
and after that there's a net of woodbine
with creamy crabs displaying their claws.
Then you'll hear water, nothing romantic,
more like the sound of kettles being filled,
and just out of earshot a sudden cottage
with roses showing half civilised faces.

For the next half mile the road will dither
till it makes up its mind to follow a trainer
and keep its eye on teams of sheep

dressed in their rival football jerseys;
then up and away it climbs again
till it reaches the uppermost shelf of the glen
where ornaments of boulders that are God's own dolmens
for the death of an age all sit secure.

Now shorten your stride to lengthen your life
and pass on your right a twist of barbed wire
like a clothes line wool-hung with rampaging attire
and you'll come to an ancient riot of rushes
secretive ferns in league with spiders
climbing clouds and kneeling bushes.

Then a startle of lark and a lick of hair
that the heather gives to a pate of rock
are the final stamps on your passport to where
the butterflies live in their last redoubt.

Get ready to smile and eyejump and shout.

For there they are like printed muslin –
scores of wings all woven together;
a school reunion for all the classes;
God's retrospective exhibition;
so many, so varied it seems as though
a lepidopterist's lost portfolio
was found here by God the Creator who yearned
to see in their lightness their calm and their sheen
what His plans for the prototype angels had been:
Hairstreak Greens and Holly Blues,

Red Admirals on their northern cruise,
thieves who've stolen Peacock feathers,
Small Heaths, Large Heaths in the heather,
Whites like fountains spurting flight,
airforce miniatures engaged in fight
insignia blazoned on their brazen wings
and flouncing Browns playing tig among the whins.

Now I've told you where the butterflies are,
so go to Donovan's Castle by car
and walk grasseasy up the middle of the road
and you'll come to the shimmering mind of God.

DIALOGUE CONCERNING THE TIMING OF A SUNBATHE

There is a time for everything
under the sun.
Is this the time for a sunbathe?

No way. The wind does not consent.
The beach flag is a stretch of red
tugging at the flagstaff like a boy
frantic to escape his lanky sister's grip.

It's struck from red to amber now.
I cannot wait for green,
I am impatient as a motorist.

No, flags aside, there is a protocol.
You can't strip till the sun strips first.
The sun is in a cummerbund
and there's another bolt of linen cloud
unwinding from the west.

Now can I peel?
The sun is now as naked as a plate!

Not yet. You cannot preach
the gospel of the sun until
his prophet, his precursor has appeared.
Look for his presence on a rock.

I see him, tip to tail
eight inches long,
tip snouting from the Nile,
tail boneless as a gymnast girl,
fingers so delicate
the rock is a piano,
and hind legs spread like anchor flukes.

That's he, the lizard, sent by God.
Prepare you now
the way of the sunbathe.

LONELINESS

In days when love painted a fixed sun
over the companionable hills
and we came to a crossroads
we tossed a coin for which way we should take
and where the smiling penny spun
like a discus out of view
we went in that direction too.

Today I followed where a slouchy shoulder led
and though it brought me thirstily
to a blue saucer on a grainy brown turf table
I knew that when I walked back to my car
I would consult an apathetic map
to find out what the overt lake was called.

In days when we surveyed the tarns of love
she would have sat upon the rippled rock
and tossed her shoes behind her like two sods
and sailed her feet like two white wherries
out and back to Schull or Skerries,
and when we found the car again
a million smiles away
we'd shut the doors upon the secret name
we gave the lake we cradled in the day.

FIRST CELL

Shrapnel of newspaper nudes
bursting from explosive walls
with breasts explicit as canted cakes
in a confectioner's.
Two saucepans without handles
for pissing in the swollen night.
Refuse squatting
in the only corner
not claimed by huddled clothes.
Kraal of toilet rolls
on the veldt of barren floor.

Myself the fearful novice
I share this cell of misery
with two professional companions.
One is a roller of self-cigarettes
who primes them like torpedo tubes
to fire at the freighter of despair;
the other crushes an accordion
between hands as large as bricks
even as he tilts a pensive head
and closes lids emotively on eyes
as though the squeals he hears are waters
from an age before the salmon knew
they could raise a flashing arch.

THE PAIN OF LOSS

If I should lose the scholars' abstract God
in the postulated life that follows this,
that pain of loss, the theologians say,
will sear the soul more than the fire
which I have scented
smouldering in their minatory books;
and in my prison hell no other pain
can match the loss of God's creative smile
patterning the earth's forbidden face.

PRISONER

Never before have I walked
under a geometric sky.
I watch the others scurry round the yard
impotent as mice
in an empty biscuit tin.

An officer, gardener from the groves
of law, dangles from his showy hand
a teasing pineapple of keys
the juice of which I shall not drink.

All the trees of Leinster have been felled
except for one the crest of which
stripped of perspective, lies, it seems,
a shapeless sponge
on top of the filthy wall,
a tree without a root or soil
for soil itself has no existence now
except on page eleven forty three
of my mutilated dictionary:
the warder in Reception sliced its covers off
like rashers off a side of ham;
with covers on, he said, it was classified
a deadly weapon in a faction fight.

I roll, I toss my heedless sleeve
to know what time it is, but all I see

is the stampede of scuttling hairs:
I have forgotten for the hundredth time
that when they clapped the handcuffs on my wrist
they took my watch away.

Only one image puts a floating hull
under the heavy bales of gloom
and that is when the slim twin stacks
of the boiler house become
twin funnels of a paddlesteamer which
are stayed to a promenaded deck
and are as bright as alder when she wheels
down Mississipi to a port of hope.

SLEEP

Sleep is the only corner of this hell
where I'm not singed by anguish.
Bed is the surgery
for the swollen tumour of the day,
the cancer caused by rubbing hides
against the other cattle that we are,
penned in the prison yard,
the growth accelerated every day
by the frenzy of the communal TV,
the inability to see
myself in any mirror that the Lord God made
and by the mocking mouths
that give a voice to uniforms.
Sleep is the only tool
can file escape
out of the cell my soul has now become.

RACING PIGEON IN THE PRISON YARD

She is there static and penally alone
before any of our conduited feet
are gated through into the yard
but when she sees the kin of creatures who
wheeled eyes for whirling wings like hers
in pigeon cities north and south of haste
she saunters towards us with bold swinging hips
down the middle of the empty boulevard.

A Corkman spots a ring and marries her
to a fancier in Mayfield or Fairhill
and with the scoop of hands
he crafted once in knee high streams
for catching sticklebacks he follows her
to read the marriage lines. A lout
shouts "Twist her neck" but he snaps back
"I'd twist yours if it weren't for the camera".

The training that the pigeon got
in architecture tells her that the rows
of small square windows, cells to us,
are a pigeon loft stopover on the flight
to home. So to evade arrest
at the hands of friendly curiosity
she tries to enter but to find
that bars of iron truly make a cage.

That's when her freedom head rejects the thought
of prison life and from the ledge she leaps
to the topmost level of the wall where coils
of razor wire roll like wheels, bright spares
for an equipe. Then cyclist lithe she springs
to a saddle that is visible to none
but to herself, and helmet headed thrusts her way
to spinning hills invisible to us.

CENSORSHIP OF LETTERS

I am handed a letter
with its white head slit open;
the censor has cleaved it
with his roistered machete.

When mailed by the sender
it was a virgin;
when it came to the censor's
the officer raped it.

Eavesdropper on friendship;
peeping tom at our river
where our words swim together
he paws at the clothing

of our intimate thinking
and I can't find a perfume
with which to deodor
the stench of intrusion.

My letters are daggered
like gullgutted mussels:
the censor's raw bill is
the first maw to gorge them.

I must hide my shelled poems
clear of his rending;

otherwise seafood verses
will be spilled out like entrails.

THE PRISON MOON

I saw the moon roasting
on the gridiron of the prison bars
and it fed me for an hour
of the famished night.

Next I saw it like a great ear.
"Listen to me, moon", I prayed,
"Christ was deafened by his own
ascension rocket on Mount Olivet
and now He doesn't hear".

And then I saw it pear
like a helium balloon
and it lifted me
above the walls, the watchtower
and the menace of the lights
to a stratosphere of calm.

UPON HEARING THAT A SPRIG OF SHAMROCK SENT TO ME BY POST HAS BEEN CONFISCATED

In their own unalterable minds
fired in the kiln of prison rules
all they have done is to invoke a law
which states no substances of any sort
may be enclosed in letters,
so they are well within their rights
to frisk the envelope addressed to me
and to expose the hidden threat
of shamrock.

But what they have done to Patrick is
they have thrown his teaching aid
more cogent than a library of tomes
into a trashcan;
and what they have done to the trefoil God
is something that the Romans dared not do:
they have pulped the legs of His only Son;
they have chopped the wings
off the Blessed Dove
stooping on its Jordan mark;
and they have scrubbed
the small echoes of the mighty Voice
that bade the vegetation to appear
on the third day of the Creator's week.

Nearer home than Trinity
they have spewed the yellow vomit
of the paraquat in their minds
over the path where Michael my old friend
picked the sprig of shamrock.
That is a path that goes two ways:
up to the hillside's holy well
above which the kestrel pins a cross
on a lapel of sky,
and down to the lake where cloistered swans
move religiously;
Patrick blessed the birds
when they were novices,
and he skimmed the coracle of his hand
across the water of the well
when it spurted a thousand gods.

If those who demonised his shamrock saw
him stooping to pick the plant on Tara
they would have cut his thumb
and index finger off
with a slash of their censor's knife.

May their children's
and their children's children's brains
be like the stomach walls
of grazing cows
unable to discriminate
between the shamrock
and mere clover!

A SORT OF CAT

The prisoner, a mate of mine,
halted on his orbit round the yard
showering the sunshine
with light droplet words.
Where he paused, my body humanised
a grey barbaric patch
of prison wall;
my face was tilted to the only warmth
in our concreted world.
"What you remind me of", he said,
"is Seán Ó Ríordáin's purring line –
an cat ag crú na gréine."

Dear God how right he was.
I was a sort of cat,
a serial number in a litter
without name or home or dignity
whose only comfort in the chill of life
is her ability to purr
when sucking at the great tit of the sun
on the rare occasion when it streams
into her cranny in the ravaged lane
where no one ever comes.

SWAN SONG

(In memoriam L.M.)

The ballad that the old man sang
"The Little Grey Home in the West"
sagged in every line
after the carry of the long long day.

When he drew breath
at the end of a phrase
the brakes in his chest shrieked.

His eyes were two round bulbs
lit by the battery
of his consumptive face.

He held the microphone in his hands
with the terminality
of a blessed candle.

All the prisoners at the concert said
the medics should be sacked
for letting him go directly
from inhaling oxygen
to exhaling life.
"He'll drop dead", we moaned
"on the climb to the next high note".

But he scaled those pulmonary heights,
and we had another five long listening nights
before the rattle in the lungs
gave way
to the rattle in the throat.

Now I know
that it was God
who was the concert impresario
and the song about the evening rest
that the old man sang
had nothing to do with the greying west.

He could see with eyes like oracles
beyond the mist of cigarettes
to where the blue shadows
of his ballad really fell.

DEUS EX MACHINA

God has come to me
quietly
by parachute

bailing out
of a flak-loud heaven

dodging all the razor wire on guard,
finding a dropzone
in the prison yard.

It was a slow descent
hampered by the hither thither
of my own uncertain weather
of indifference

and because when I briefed God
about my rescue route
I said no word
about a silent parachute.

I specified that He
should dart in noisily
with the infinitely grand
gesture of a helicopter, land,
scoop me aboard, then vault
the merely human walls

and find a helipad of liberty.

But He did not appear
under the spinning halo of bright blades
which means He cannot now propel
Himself back to the godosphere.

No, He has stepped
out of the harness straps
and come to my astonished cell
where we will share a single fetter
which is, Paul the apostle says, far better.

...EXCEPT THAT I'M NOT THERE

The inlet at Goleen is smooth and clean
as a child's tongue, and the heron pans
among the shallows like a veteran,
and at the quay the wetted steps
measure the power of the moon
and the small boats rub their hips
together, and the quay itself is a paradise
of untidiness with ropes and boxes everywhere,
and the tide, the mosaic maker, has arranged
its tesserae of broken shells
upon the shore. Nothing has changed
except that I'm not there.

The Ilen river endlessly flirts
with the road to Aughadown, alongside which
the foxgloves raise their totem poles
and the promontory church is a ship
high and dry in a dock, and a fox
moves like the fastener of a zip
through the green fabric of the fields
and a Little Egret long estranged
from her Spanish kin treads Irish pools,
and six bullocks with one dismissive stare
secure a gate. Nothing has changed
except that I'm not there.

The cat crouches in her rhubarb ambuscade

in Ella's garden, and the apple trees
are planeted with red and green
and mottled worlds; the sweetpeas masquerade
as butterflies and the garden seat
is sacred to the memory of Hakan's nodding head;
the gladiolas draw their swords and spread
their banners and the climbing roses map
a delta; fuchsias brag of the despair
of jewellers, and kittens are deranged
by their gyrating tails. Nothing has changed
except that I'm not there.

TWO SUMMERS I HAVE LOST

Two summers I have lost
at what a cost
to ear and eye!

A kestrel's fingers splayed
on piano, played
in quavering sky.

Full spinnakers in blows
bent like drawn bows:
wind's tournament.

The cuckoo's June decoy,
his trickster joy,
fools further sent.

Mountains in clannish crowds,
and clannish clouds
their traffic signs.

Round bales of August straw
like panzers drawn
in battle lines.

The hour when impish sun
sticks out his tongue
at Oileán Clear.

Two summers I have lost
at what a cost
to eye and ear!

LEPER MASS

"You may say Mass," the bishop said,
"but never again in a church",
which means I can swim in a fishtank
but never again in the sea;
I can climb a pair of steps
to fetch preserves in jars
but not a hill
to stud the night with stars.

The cubby where I offer Mass
I call the leper hole
because no healthy eyes must see
the silver hourglass
filled with eternity,
or hear the slow drip of the sacred words.
Sometimes I wonder whether God Himself
will stoop upon my hidden offerings
for I have neither aisle nor transept where
He'd spread His awesome and enormous wings.

"The Lord be with you" I say to walls.
In the mirror of my heart I cannot tell
if what I wear to greet the deaf and dumb
is leper poncho or a chasuble.
The Christ I know lives gaunt, alone,
within the wilderness that is my Mass
and speaks to nothing but to stone.

There are no fish, no boats, no bread, no grass,
there are no people, there is no oasis.
I lift the white Moon of the sunken sun,
bright Host, but light no galaxy of faces,
and not a prayer ends with Amen Amen:
they all end with the cry "Unclean. Unclean."

STORIES

THE WELL AT PAMPAMARCA

At Pampamarca there is a spring
that never in a thousand summers
baked cakes of clay.

Always it leaped laughing
over the shoulders of the naked pitchers
when they plunged into the well.

In the annals of a hundred trowels
no mason ever nudged
a wall to stand around it.

This was because the sacred apu Imla
who was born of the well womb
and tiptoed on the bedrock,

whose darting eyes like waterbeetles
moved in the socket of the surface
loved to see his devotees approach

with their filial offerings of thirst.
Not for him to live unseeing
blinded by a garrison of stone.

Then a new alcalde from the north
Pablo Cesar del Ocururo,
raised in the new religion of improvements,

ordered the well to be enclosed.
But through the final gap of light
before investment was complete

the apu Imla led the water like a snake
out beneath the hissing sun
writhing to the burying sands.

In Inca times when the apu of a well
evacuated all his waterfolk
and left a town's throat dry

they would induce him to return
with a bribe of human blood,
a young girl lissom as a brook

or a boy as daring as a waterfall.
So Pampamarca, Incan in its drought
but Christian in its children's shoes,

looked for a surrogate for innocence
and found it in their municipal fool
Toribio, wayward as a flood.

He used to climb the pulpit preaching giggles,
he'd sit a mule with tail for reins
he'd limp on broken wings of rags

and everyday his name bounced off their tongues
but when the fight came between laughs and water

the water won the bloody bout.

One morning when the priesting sun
tilted a full chalice at the town
a shepherd found Toribio at the well

his throat knifed through, his snaking blood
making for shelter in the empty trough.
And on the third day the water rose again.

LORD VENTRY'S HORSES

When Lord Ventry's highborn horses
were paraded up the village street
on their way to the sacred rite
of shoeing at the forge
the tradesmen were summoned to their doors
by hooves. There they had to stand,
their hats great badges of submission
clamped to their chests. If not,
the grooms' crisscrossing eyes
became the bailiff's mouth
and the unthatchable skies
their next damp tenancy.

Only one man in all the bitter doors
looked at the spectacle;
the other heads all sagged
on passive thumbs. That man was Danny Fitz
the tailor, and although his trade had bent
his head those forty stooping years
to fingers and to cloth
he always raised his eyes with true respect
to Ventry's horses: "they are" he said
"the only beings pacing the Estate
dressed in nobility
and there's not a thimbleful of blood in them
that came from English heat".

SILENCED PRIEST

It was no surprise to anyone
when the bishop kicked away
the shaky steps to Fr. Larry's tub,
the pulpit in his portly shape,
because he spoke from there in many tongues
distilleried rather than divine,
and the titter from the chapel seats
were loud enough to span the width
of fourteen buffer parishes
and shake the righteous window sashes
in His Lordship's moated house.

Six years he wore the bishop's gag
until the diocese of death
silenced him completely,
but in those final years
he spoke another tongue,
the second language of the rustic Christ
vowels of pliant fingers
and consonants of cures.

A penny doctor he certified himself,
a tinker priest was all he claimed to be
but in the ponytrap that belled boreens
he carried solder for misshapen limbs
tinsmithery of healing touch;
he lifted blinds

on darkening rooms of eyes
he reddened little peisaun cheeks,
he flooded estuaries of ebbing lungs.

All that was fact, but to authenticate
this thaumaturgy in the minds of those
whose expectation of an Irish saint
was that he leap a waterfall
on a rainbow horse or sail to Rome
in a hull hacked out of stone,
they invested Fr. Larry in a tale
that mortified the clerical establishment.

It went like this.
Once at a conference
when fifty priests bloated as bollards
in winter clothes came to the bishop's house
they smothered the pallid entrance hall
under a weight of wool; the newel disappeared
beneath a rugby scrum of overcoats;
a dozen gabardines sat side saddle on
the banisters, and the hallstands canted
like pregnant gladiolas come to term.
Larry arrived the last of last
and finding neer a berth for his old cloak
as green as cabbage, he saw a beam
of smooth white light being levered by the sun
in through an upper window and he slung
his cloak over its carpentry,
and there above the chagrin of their eyes

greenwinged it hung
a great bird in a sky unknown to them.

ALBAN ON CUTHBERT

I am the hinges on the abbey door;
it hangs its greetings and goodbyes on me
so Brother Porter is my ranking name,
but when our annual patron draws the ale
and Father Abbot's cartwheel eyes
roll on trite badinage
they call me Brother Nightwatch.
That is mere uncorked jealousy not wit
for it was I not they who heard
our Cuthbert chant the otter vigil.

When compline snuffed out candled day
and all the brethren celled, as I supposed,
I locked my duty's great oak door;
then as I walked the passageway of dusk
I heard the bolt being drawn again,
I heard a question clanging in our hush.
When I reached the door and looked outside
the answer flowed in Cuthbert's robe,
the robe plunged downhill to the stream;
I followed, cautious tributary.

He lifted off his worsted tent,
became a tentpole on the gaping bank
then waded to a pool of modesty,
and there for hours, his head like offering
on the flow's smooth plate, he stood and prayed and sang

the psaltery of water, air and flesh
with fluting otters until dawn
lifted the sky upon a wedge of light
and out he came and knelt upon the grass
with arms that pleaded like a cormorant's.

Two otters beached and bounded to his side:
they blew white love at purpled feet, and curled
around his body with their towelling.
Then warm and dry he pressed his blessed thumb
upon their heads, and robed, and climbed the slope.
My legs were limp with wonder; he outpaced
me to the door. I knocked. He drew the bolt.
"Alban, have you been vigiling?" he asked,
"What have you heard?"
"A whirlpool of song"
"What have you seen?"
"Two angels with webbed feet".

"AMONGST THOSE WHO ATTENDED THE BURIAL WAS HER SON"

There were four locked doors
between him and the ward
where his mother sat
for twenty five uncushioned years
out of his sight
out of her mind.

Duty would have breached the outer door
which guarded the drugged silences
from the city noises;
pity, the second to the Female Block;
gratitude, the third to the Longterm Floor
where all the inmates slept
on mattresses of fetid calendars;
and love the fourth door to her vacant face
but in none of the locks did he turn a key.
Ever.

He had his reasons, sound ones naturally.
She wouldn't know him, so why shout his name
as a password to the deaf
sentry at the entrance of her mind?
Nor would he recognise her as the mother who
brushed his schoolboy hair with hands
that had no bristles.
Those were the reasons, sound ones naturally.

The years grew longer and so did his cars
and if the number plate of his ascendant Merc
should shout his Dublin Four address
to other visitors, the azulejo tiles
of his outdoor swimming pool would crack
and the water of his tropical repute
drain all away.
Death he could look at for it couldn't be
nearly as repulsive as insanity.

In spite of which he did not go
to the removal of her slight remains
because the mortuary was inside the walls
and that was foreign territory
for which he'd need a visa stamped with love;
and neither did he furniture the church
at Mass, for steps and pillars, balustrade and dome
would build a courthouse in his mind
and he might hear the words "How do you plead?"
so he went only to the burial.

From years of practice in judicious cemeteries
he knew how to comport himself
at the graveside of a distant corpse:
a well cut suit was de rigueur,
one stood in waxen silence
and showed no flicker of a feeling eye.
Then when the decade of the Rosary
gave unofficiating voices words
about the now, about the hour of death

he walked away
to where he'd parked the isolated Merc
a hundred metres from the mourning gate.

WORLD WITH AN END

(i)
THE DONOVANS OF DUNKELLY

The Donovans were as old as spit
as tough as seals
as full and plenty as an autumn pit
as lively as a landlord's wheels.

Their men were hefty, hewn of myth:
trunks of trees they had for torsos;
their women slim as herring brith –
breeding makes the best of corsets.

They drank of God, their ancient brew
(the devil was a bastard)
They knew truly what they knew:
(and left the rest to the Master)

a horse's eye, the trim of boat,
sea the wildest stallion,
the amber song of whiskey punch in throat,
blood the thickest, best battalion.

Their meadows were circuses sounding with hooves
and below was a bay of ditches
and riding the seine into cuases and coves
was rougher than saddles on breeches.

They broke horses with an eye of power,
a rope of skill;
no Donovan would ever cower
before a pounding will

but God's green eye they never would outface
on a blaspheming deck:
no impious man of theirs would place
a bridle on the sea's neck.

(ii)
DUNMANUS BAY

Behind Dunkelly where they clanned
was pagan Púca's mountain:
hardy imp he was
with green socks covering his shins
but not another stitch of grass on him
from his knees to his shaven poll.
Father O'Mahony in the Holy Year
forced him to abdure his heathen ways
and placed a pitch pine cross upon his head
but he apostatised one stormy night!

Manus of the Castle named their bay
and all around the mountains dipped
their mouths into its drinking trough.
The snuggest cove adjacent to their feet
was Canty's Cove beloved of gannets
and it was there they put their boats to bed.

Northeastwards on the water, low and black,
four islands, like an otter bitch at dawn
and her three cubs, swam in a line astern:
great Carbery leathered with bullocks for the fair
and Losc and Furze and Meenteen limed with spray.
Another island westwards screeched its name
while you were still a half a cable clear:
the gulls rose up and screamed of privacy
like German settlers nigh their coastal eggs

stridulous, distrustful and unwelcoming.

Muintir Bháire north across the bay
had small pale houses primrosing the year.
There lived the men who launched on Sunday nights
and fished in God's preserves of water
so they were meshed forever in the curse of dogfish.
Further north was Beara with a wall of sky
yielding no entry to a climbing eye
and rows and rows of low brown hills
like freshly earthed potato drills.

(iii)
THE PATRIARCH

Danny Donovan's crusty bread
came wrapped in scales;
his sovereigns bore the images
of fishes' heads and tails,
but he was not a man
who totted life by fishcount.
Sunday night he was a chatelain
and his cottage was a castle;
the sixty knees that touched his floor
were thirty of them Christian, thirty vassal.
When Danny spoke, his tongue became a gavel:
then the matchmaking had to stop
halfway through the counting of cattle,
and only the canary in the cage
could antiphone the vespers of the sage.

When he climbed down from his prophetic loft
his face was bright with godlight
and the great Book in his leather hands
was awesome as the stone of God's commands.
Not casually on one knee
as if to tie the laces on their boots
but with a total weight of fear
when mosesed Danny Donovan appeared
the revellers knelt down.

Danny put a furzebush on the fire;

it burnt with bible crackle, and the floor
clean and sanded became holy ground.
His boots came off, his eyes were on the stand,
he put the Book down lightly
the Book of prayer encased in oxhide lightly
like a currach grounding on a quiet strand.

Then Danny's homespun altarboy,
Dave Sullivan, stood on a solemn chair
and lit two candles eitherside of prayer.
A scamp he was and often with an eye
upon the bulge in Danny's appled smock
he turned the pages two at a craving time;
three even, it is said, if a pack of cards
slipped off the old unstable dresser
and caused the fall with swift exciting ease
of four right famous ancient dynasties.

A little baffled by this shift of wind
a little doldrummed in the holy welter
the old man kept his bearing on his God
until he berthed in the final page's shelter.
Then, 'spite of a fiddle yielding to a yawn,
he kept his Maker wakeful to his words
in trimmings stitched upon his faith and hope
reminding Him of Massachusetts kin,
of mourning eyes with curtains drawn,
of lissom bones beneath the sod
west in Kilmoe, bad Bantry rope,
the peevish nature of the year's sciollán,

wily fish, the price of salt, unruly water.
A sick mare
got the final fondle of a special prayer.
And then he bellowed "Agnes!"
(Agnes was his daughter)
"Stretch out your prim accordion
and give some tune a roast
in the name of the Father and of the Son
and of the Holy Ghost."

(iv)
THE MUSICIAN

When she played for the dancers after Sunday suppers
their shoes drew breath by parting soles from uppers.
She will be remembered for the shirts that rotted
and the hearts that raced like wristlet watches.

The master of ceremonies was her cigarette:
the match that lit it primed the kitchen set,
and as the smoke invested hair and head
her "Siege of Ennis" butchered dying and dead.

No lull or parley came to feet or hips
until her Gold Flake seared her own clenched lips
and then the squeeze box squealed with pain,
the set collapsed, the doors burst open under strain
and the saints upon the dresser became themselves again.

(v)
CHANGED TIMES

Everything changed.
The hillsides, glossy and curved
like well fed cats, picked up a mange.
Only the road and the house stayed young:
the road tirelessly hide-and-seeking play among
the trusty ever-secretive boulders
and the thatch on the house falling like a schoolboy's fringe
over a pale washed forehead and paint-blue eyes;
everything else got old and older.

The mackerel left.
There were no more phosphorescent nights
when the moon threw sugar on the fire
and the fish blazed;
no more historical encirclements;
the thousands became mere hundreds
and the hundreds learnt the trick of flight.
The women put away their gutting knives
like Amazons sadly
after the last exterminating battle.
The nets were hung like webs
above the dewy shore
but the spiders mended them no more
and all those great percussion bands of barrels
drumming on the skirted quay
dispersed.

The English steamer
for years familiar as a local boy
with its empty stomach
and its kite of smoky joy
sailed off forever to another pickled sea.
The young men followed her to Liverpool and there
they took the westward Packet to despair
and in its wake the ancient ways were swamped.

The sun kept low in the old men's sky;
stakes they made of oars.
The wind pushed in the doors.
In Lackavaun there was a shelf
of hill where in the dresser days
the houses shone like delf;
now they stared like shrunken skulls.

Danny died.
There was no fishing crew
upon a day of meditative haze
and responsorial gulls
to shoulder him with sea-lope to Kilmoe.
And in the Cove, beloved of gannets,
the seine boats of Dunkelly rotted
like carcasses of sheep upon a fevered hill
their black ribs skeletons of a forgotten skill.

(vi)
LAST OF THE LINE

Agnes too grew old.
The hanging hair of youth
wayward as a waterfall
was disciplined by age's art and rolled
up, like a temple capital with volutes.
Seldom you saw it Grecian: her black shawl
of an Irish storm cloud covered all.
The coffins for her menfolk came and went,
green timber for the seasoned bones
and the Mass-going mare was sold;
so at the last, the last of the Donovans
walked the obedient road
to Sunday, bent
by the weight of the sodden miles.

What of it? In Goleen the children's smiles
lightened the lonely road.
To see a ring of them was an atoll
enclosing life's lagoon of sighs.
Children were her alcohol:
she drank them craving with her eyes.
They set her purse on fire;
givishness and love were her Brigade;
she put the fire out with lemonade.
"Well, God be praised for Sunday" she always said.

For till it came again her childless chairs

were like stopped clocks
(one time the legs that swung from them
were pendulums in frocks)
and all those cruel weekdays would condemn
her, ageing, to behold
her accordion co-conspirator and friend
hanging from a butcher's hook, contorted, cold,
her minstrel dead beneath the silent stairs.

(vii)
LONELIEST OF DEATHS

Agnes in her turn died:
the adage "As you live, so will you ..." lied.
In the house where forty four
danced blood one night from the flayed floor
she died alone.
There was no one with her to heat the stone
of chill, to sun the lamp,
to flood the drought of lips, to flex the cramp
of childlessness, no one at all
to scale the mountain with a Christian call
for priest, for Oils, for Wafered way
to God there walking on the Bay,
no one awake to sleep her face,
no prayerbook to exorcise the mouth's grimace,
no friend to draw a friend's disguise
over the terror in her sightless eyes.

They brought the doctor then to quarry in her corpse;
their minds took hold of warps
to tow her small abandoned ship to port;
and at the wake they tried to thaw the thought
of cold neglect with tea and turf briquettes;
then bought the cheapest coffin they could get
for a woman who enriched a thousand pasts.
Money crumbles, goodness lasts.
The priest was frightful angry, so 'twas said.
Anger is the best of tributes to the dead.

ISBN 1-41206404-X